SEVENTY-TWO LABORS

SEVENTY-TWO LABORS

poems

Susan KōDō Efird

Antrim House

Bloomfield, Connecticut

Library of Congress Control Number: 2022912451

ISBN: 979-8-9855621-7-0

First Edition

Printed & bound by Ingram Content Group

Book design by Rennie McQuilkin

Cover photograph by Karin Halvorson Hillhouse
(Kojokan Gate to upper garden, Saihoji,
designed by Musō Soseki, Kyoto, Japan)

Author photograph by Karin Hillhouse

Antrim House
860.217.0023
AntrimHouseBooks@gmail.com
www.AntrimHouseBooks.com
400 Seabury Dr., #5196, Bloomfield, CT 06002

For Karin

companion, reader, navigator

A NOTE ABOUT THE TITLE

"Seventy-two labors" refers to the Zen chant recited before meals. Here's how the chant begins: "First, seventy-two labors brought us this food. We should know how it comes to us." In a traditional Japanese monastery seventy-two service positions, from abbot to novice, assured its simple and peaceful functioning. "Labors" is also translated as offerings or gifts, so the chant affirms the generosity of those who helped prepare our meal.

Seventy-two labors is a metaphor for the interconnection of all lives, sentient and insentient. In the food we eat we experience the presence of countless worlds supporting us. The sun, rain, the earth and its nutrients. The seeds and the farmers and all that inspires the life of a farmer. Pollinators, sprinklers, combines, truck drivers, and everything that sustains them. Those who construct the electrical grid and maintain it. The grocery store clerks, the light fixtures, floorboards, and forced-air coolers. The delivery persons.

Put simply, *Seventy-Two Labors* expresses gratitude for the forces close around and far beyond us. That network of beings past, present, and future makes possible not only our nourishing meals but also every wonder of our very lives. And we, in turn, appreciate and nurture life.

TABLE OF CONTENTS

Who can know what is sacred and what is ordinary?
    –Zen Master Dogen, *Instructions for the Cook*

SEVENTY-TWO LABORS

THE POTS AND PLATES OF EVERY DAY

The Pots and Plates of Every Day

For my mother

"Wonderful! Wonderful! The preaching of the Dharma
by the nonsentient is inconceivable," exclaims Dongshan.
–Zen Master Keizan, *The Record of Transmitting the Light*

Gather round and share this meal
Your joy and your sorrow I make mine.
– The Gate of Sweet Nectar

I

The pot fills me with wonder.
Open and empty like the sky,
it shares its upright heart.
It cannot turn away from hunger—
always its hand reaches out
like the sun or gusting wind.
No one is turned away,
it is born to serve.

Scorched black and cinnamon
on the bottom, and inside
scoured paths of shooting stars,
outside, the pot glints silver
like rain through sun in summer,
its wooden handle worn from
decades of dedicated work—
how radiant the pot awake
on the stove.

Sharing its mineral life with mountains,
the pot echoes their daring of distance after distance
and feeds the hungry in every realm.
The pot is pressed into service on stoves
in homes, hospitals, and prisons
or over campfires after a day's trek
with many fleeing violence or drought.
Always moving toward the fire
the pot offers the warmth
and savor of being alive,
of sharing a meal.

Within the pot hot water for tea
or nutty oatmeal, earthy lentils or black
beans with garlic, steaming broccoli,
fragrant soup, sautéing onions,
boiling corn, or steeping broth.
The pot nurses us in illness and health,
putting food in the bellies of the wise
and foolish, the kind and the unkind.
The pot's reassuring hand will shake
all others' and give comfort.

Dinner is ready!

Come and receive the cosmos itself.
Within the pot not only vegetables
and grains but the earth and sky
that grew them—the red sun of summer,
the sheening rains of autumn,
the embrace of snow bearing eons
of silence and absence, the revelations

of moonlight with plants waving like oceans
tugged by tides and the spring star Arcturus
illuminating and enriching the topsoil
mentored by a chilled earthworm
which imparts its brilliance, then snugs
up to an onion bulb and falls asleep.
The joyful pot holds the whole of life.

II

The pot sees clearly what needs
to be done but it cannot provide solace
alone. Another, sleeves rolled up,
must take its hand for cooking to begin.
The pot lives by trust and glows
like the moon by reflected light
patient and mysterious
on the white stove of everyday life.

The wooden spoon on the table,
the pot's companion, open as a palm
and like the pot reaching out,
must also wait for another.
More ancient than fork or knife
and more gentle, the slender spoon
lathed from beech and lightly stained
with turmeric brims with invention,
never weary, making the meal—
offering its dance to the pot and
joining hands with its partner.

Close by, knobs of garlic nod delight
and sinuous salt and pepper
sentinels gather their wits.

The pot's eternal calling is imbued with humor—
it is after all only a pot, and unadorned,
disappearing into service. Laughing at itself
the pot calls out to those in need
of conversation and laughter
to keep their meals warm.

III

The pot devotes itself to every cook.

A cashier at a casino who lost
her job fixes dinner for her girls
a soup her mother made—fried pasta shells,
tomato sauce, diced tomatoes, and water.
The younger child sets out a bowl and
spoon for her dreadlocked doll who loves
the ceremonies of daily life.

Thinning gray hair, masked, the sous-chef
in a hospital kitchen boils spaghetti
in huge pots for staff treating
Covid patients. Outside, a refrigerated
truck serves as neighborhood morgue.
Seeing faces exhausted beneath
shields, he bows his head and weeps.

A boy named Lucky, youngest of four,
breaking from his online class,
stirs a simple syrup for lemonade.
Ill with cancer, his mother reads aloud
the recipe and watches lemons roll
like small suns across the long maple island
in that never-ending moment with her son.

Escaping drought, crops ruined,
they stop for a break on the outskirts
of a town after finding no food
and heat water for coffee.
Backpacks for pillows,
he, his wife, and their girl Rosa
rest before resuming their route,
hoping for food tomorrow.
Their life on the road toward life
is replete only with tomorrows.

A man at Eastham, a Texas prison,
prays for the well-being of the cook
who heated his green beans and hot dog.
That's better than some folks get,
he thinks, but the cockroaches—
I know them have joys and sadness.
Coaxing one to leave his cell,
he tells her, "But wrong house,
go next door. Sh-h-h-h-h!
Dakota don't need to know."

Late at night an elderly woman scoops
water from the basement as a gale batters
her house. A sleeve on her knee since
the last hurricane. Now, a tropical storm
brewing. The swaying bulb blinks out.
Light is exhausted too, she thinks, and
feels her way upstairs. She finds the pot
waiting on the stove. Maybe creamed
spinach tomorrow.

At a shelter the man cleaning a pot
watches as men eat their oatmeal
then begin to go separate ways.
The last to leave, a carpenter, his tools
stolen from his truck, then the truck
stolen. Carrying a frayed blanket,
he hunts for cardboard to sleep
on that night. "Just help me,"
he prays. "Ok? Just a little?"

Somewhere in heaven Miss Cissy
cooks chicken stew for her son George.
"You were there for me," he says.
"I heard you call out—I'm not far away.
I put fresh sheets on your bed.
George, before we eat say a prayer."
"Dear God thank you for our breaths
which nothing can extinguish
and for this hearty food."
They gaze out over the many hands
stretching down to connect with

the hands of those jailed and those still
marching, until they finally return
home and reheat leftovers for dinner.
Miss Cissy smiles at her son George Perry.
"Please pass the stew," he says.

IV

Distressed that so many have little food
the pot sighs an endless aspiration to feed everyone—
the scared the left behind those alone
families in line in cars for hours at food banks
those without cars or meals
their frightened children
ICU patients starved for life
others starved for love or justice
the ravaged planet itself.

Intensifying its efforts the pot unfolds
a thousand arms, praying that sustenance
for everyone be expanded beyond measure.
Taking a hand we shake hands
with everything that is and together
watch for the stove's coiled lightning.
The pot fires its iron roots—stars
combusting into being after the Big Bang—
both heaven and earth heat the green beans
and chicken stew and the glorious, plentiful food.

V

Near the window on the white counter
the pot recuperates with friends
in the early morning. Listening
like a valley, the pot fills with birdsong
and the high notes of the coreopsis.
And the sounds of pebbles alive—
their pebble hands shining
with the enduring strangeness of clouds.

And inside, from the cutting board
with incised verticals like sheeting
rain a soothing thrumming.
From the green ancestral branches
of the spoon rustlings above
the forest floor just waking up.
The kitchen walls in lacquered
shadow sing by gleaming.
The hint of songs of pots
and pebbles, cutting boards, and spoons.

Just when we do not speak but slip free
of thinking and sentience
we begin to hear the inconceivable
music of the insentient—
their no striving after movement or gain,
the elegance of nothing extra
in a culture addicted to more,
their ebullient service to life and
wondrous receptivity to being,
their beyond human teaching.

This silence of wisdom and ease
emanates from the pot and its friends
near the patio and in the small kitchen
at the blue nearing of dawn.

VI

I watch bubbles skip above the singing
water, pot ablaze, as steam rises
framing my face. With ready intent
and hungry, I pour lentils into the reeling
cauldron then seize the comet spoon and stir.
The woman feeding her family pasta soup
and the man in solitary eating his beans
and praying for the cook—how are they?
I cover the simmering pot and wait.

A great mix of ingredients is poured
into pots around the world. Magnanimous
as the ocean the pot welcomes everything,
then delivers the bounty wholeheartedly.
In this day-to-day life on a minor spiral arm
of the Milky Way and Sagittarius A* which houses
our little corner of Earth and sun and stars,
I soon uncover the pot then sit down
to my lunch of lentils and thyme.

VII

Seeing the pot reach out we see who we are
and at once reach out to those who hunger in any form.
We reach out to the shattered, the struggling.
We reach out to workers without work
freezing at home without heat or prospect.
We reach out to the old, dying without
human touch or the gaze of a familiar face.
We reach out to dying rhinos, red wolves,
and wetlands lost to parking lots.

As we reach out we see that others
are also reaching out, bestowing gifts.
Why had we not seen this before?

The drift of seas affirms the drift of seasons.
The mountains of Earth fade into emptiness
shoring up the mountains of Mars. Our warm stoves
revive our wider home, our warm bridge
of stars. Shadows mirror light
at play in unceasing creation.

VIII

All of life brings forth life and possibility—
even a virus quickens compassion.
Is there anything that is not alive and
utterly generous? Braided as one
sentient and insentient, indistinguishable.

We throw open doors and floors, tear off the roof
pull down the open sky and let life stream in.
We are the pots, the pebbles, and the poise
of cutting boards, and they are us—
the oneness of our ordinary lives
originating in the stars.

IX

Together we prepare the supreme meal
for each other, holding back nothing.
We draw on even our fears and darkness,
our limitations, as a blade of grass
shares shadows and a hill its loneliness.
With courage and kindness like the pot
we sustain and encourage life.

Whatever food satisfies our longings
whatever succor the flower or street requires
we offer and receive from one another.
Quiet in mystery, our timeless origins
ignite the light and code of existence,
embedding in the DNA of every emerging
cell of our vast connected life compassion.
We are the love the universe pours into us
and into the pots and plates of every day.

We take our places at the table.
Even the freshening wind sits down with us.
We dine on a feast of every taste and texture.

Led by birds, songs praise this meal of meals
which resolves every thirst and hunger.
As we savor the best wine from the Big Dipper
perfectly aged over billions of years, we share
our joys and sorrows and deep gratitude.
Laughter rises like a spring of life-weaving waters.

The unsurpassable peace of pots.

SONG CYCLES

Translating the Wind

A wind stirs.
Ah, this world, that world.
–Ko Un, 108 Zen Poems

The bird trilled
and the dog barked.
Then the dog trilled
and the bird barked
curious about the other.
So glad to have met.

*   *   *

This morning
as a guest of the road
I heard it say
Hold on to nothing.

*   *   *

A moment in March
buffeting and ever green
flashing coins of
sunlight and wind, wind
and shivering sun, sway
and rush of wind I refresh
as tree.

*   *   *

Singing and singing
the solitary bird
a stream stops
to listen.

*   *   *

Engulfed in the distant
bass of the approaching
squall I hear the soft
scrape of rain
drops
hitting
the sidewalk.

*   *   *

Inhaling
exhaling
following the breeze
no one knows
where we go.

*   *   *

On the bus to NY
the woman in front
of me at the end of
her book. "Conclusion,"
it reads. What conclusion?
Even death's not a given,
only opening after
opening.

*   *   *

Sharing life
the roots of trees
for centuries
pump water and sugars
to the ancient stump
of a felled beech.
I breathe in
and you breathe out.
Shorebirds breathe in
and oceans let go.

*   *   *

Friend behind bars
in Raleigh for forty
years, your remains
milk-white ash
and glints of bone
like broken shells—
from the shore
of what moons?

*   *   *

Roar of a plane overhead
a bird begins to sing.
A woman on the plane
hears the brown thrasher
she heard long ago.

*   *   *

How can I face
the serviceberry blooming
so early? The sparrows
dust bathing in empty
flowerpots on the porch?
How few we are
say the birds.

*   *   *

The rain of an early
spring glisten-
ing like dew
falls without
falling.

*   *   *

The flowering cherries at dusk—
are they basking in Saigyō's
aching affection for them
during his lonely wanderings
until he died as he had hoped
under a full moon
with Yoshino trees in bloom?

*   *   *

Every moment is spring and
opens into bloom in every realm.
Every moment is new and offered

~22~

fearlessly. The suffering world is healed
by freshness. I saw it for the first time—
a branch of spring.

*   *   *

Birdsong before dawn—
silence or song?

*   *   *

A bird's high-pitched
staccato
bursts
of
day
break.

*   *   *

Forks play
with the setting sun, plates
orbit the wind. A meal
with someone we love.
The table is set above
the earth and
above the heavens.

*   *   *

Spring holds up
torches of flowers
and trees—
we make our way.

*   *   *

Weary from travel I scatter
your ashes under a young oak.
We leave together on the breeze.

*   *   *

Close to the breath
I've forgotten my name.
Any name will do,
something silly.

*   *   *

Daffodils in pouring rain
all point down,
startled to see the grass
for the first time
and the grass surprised too
smiles at the flowers.

One Two Three Four

–Musō Soseki, *Sun at Midnight*

Dreaming I was breathing
in and breathing out
rouses me from sleep

upright in the dark
astonished
this breathing in
and breathing out
no one
is breathing.

*   *   *

Sailing out,
the sky at my feet
and above my head
the long-winged wind.

*   *   *

Ghost
geese
head
south
in

fraying
autumn
honks
caught
on fog.

* * *

The road shivers into a river
of yellow leaves while high above,
the cold ginkgo with its exposed
branches braces a bird's nest
still promising life.

* * *

Our lives the ideal
distance from the sun
stall with plastic and heat.
We are consumed by grief.

* * *

The junco rests
near the curb, breast
still plump, but the eyes
are white. *Now what?*
inquires the bird
to the everlasting
changing sky.

* * *

Breath catches on breath—
what chasms between us
in this cheerless country.
Light years apart from one
another do the stars know
profound sadness too?

*   *   *

My hands like two leaves
open and extended
in these convulsive times
must cling to nothing
and do what they can.

*   *   *

Swirling leaves stop to talk
on the sidewalk. Bamboos lean
forward to hear. A cloud
becomes an ear.
What's the latest?

*   *   *

If we lose green
can we endure
its complement—
red sedges and trees
and shrubs, the color
of Earth on fire?

*   *   *

Marveling over books on Zao Wou-Ki—
a galaxy in every oil and India ink.
Now "Red and Black Sky,"
a small lithograph for my birthday,
a billion suns pull down heaven
over an untroubled planet.

*   *   *

Preschoolers holding a light rope
with teachers at each end trail
through the neighborhood, their eyes
and ears waking, while one child
hangs back and an aide takes his
trusting hand and walks with him.
Will he be the one in school gunned
down next week?

*   *   *

Standing still, the sun abbreviates the night
and yet trumped-up charges
savage the other.
More light is offered
but still we are
blind.

*   *   *

Every morning in the *Wash
Post*, between the weather and
the date, newsprint staining

my fingers, I underscore
the words *Democracy Dies
in Darkness*.

*   *   *

Breathing in the limitless world
and breathing out this world without limit
I scramble eggs for our breakfast.

*   *   *

Listening
spacious
to one another
and round
with a reach like the sea.

*   *   *

Companions for so long
we've grown old together—
how tender the unknown.

*   *   *

One two three four . . .
two hands ten fingers
I counted them as a child
and as a woman of sixty and nine
I count again and am happy.

*   *   *

Even tables breathe. We breathe in
their breath, and tables breathe

into their lungs our breath, and meteors
also inhale the special life of tables, and

table lungs the patient breath of meteors,
then slowly exhale into the shared air.

The gap between the inhalation and
exhalation—

what is this pause?

*　　*　　*

I look in the mirror but who
peers back? A whale?
A flagman? Arctic lichen?
Washing my face, combing
my hair, who are you
here before me?

*　　*　　*

By day the sun celebrating light
and by night the cloud-singed moon.
Do we see more clearly
in the dark, our eyes adjusting
to what can never be known?

Generous the Moment

Ah!
The first snow
of a mild winter
silence
over
come
by
silence.

*   *   *

A congregation of snowflakes
lies down, surrendering
into light,
reminding us
we are one.

*   *   *

Can I soften the fist of my heart
toward my numberless selves—
the clerk behind the corner deli
who insults women, the young neighbor
who disparages Jews, the arsonist
of the flame-gutted Joshua trees?

*   *   *

I cannot stop gazing at Kannon,
this carved figure after Enku
of the Bodhisattva of Compassion
who calls forth aspiration
to protect the broken
Earth and suffering beings.

*   *   *

Everything is given.
Only when
we give
can we taste it.
Only when we
launch ourselves
like birds
thriving on air.

*   *   *

Trees find their way under foreboding sky cliffs.
We walk with them and on our return
our now luminous
home welcomes us back.

*   *   *

Particles and waves of light
from before our birth and death
blaze through our limbs our hands
our feet and bellies, our ears, our lungs,
yet we treat each other with so little respect.

*   *   *

Four years boring
into the top of my head
with increasing intensity,
meditative energy,
my teacher concludes.
At the same time
four years of back trouble
numb feet and ankles.
What a strange creature
numb and alive.

*   *   *

Awaiting spinal surgery in a stall
beside a woman missing
a disc in her neck.
Here we are—cervical and lumbar—
one person healing together.

*   *   *

My life is not my own—
it is borrowed from
the blackened surface of a cast-iron pan
the dreams of a man who just died by gunshot
a hungry child in the Bronx
the light of Jupiter's seventy-nine moons
a clothes hanger fallen from
the trash, a decomposing leaf.

*   *   *

Spicy bean stew with cauliflower,
dinner for you on New Year's.
Afterward you thank me and
mention I used the wrong pot.
Laughter rings in the New Year!

*   *   *

Through the afternoon
window cobblestones of
clouds mortared with navy
sky move west above winter
trees. Who passes through
that gateless gate?

*   *   *

Seventy-one years
little sense of oceans
of days
only extraordinary
ordinary life.

*   *   *

In winter twilight, raindrops
drum the windshield of the bus
as we slog our way south on I-
95 to DC in dense traffic.
Facets of amethyst, scarlet, and pearl.
Their songs startle the heart.

*   *   *

Grass gives to the hopefulness of chairs
chairs to the contentment of rivers
rivers to the shimmer of every day;
drying our dishes adds vigor to tall pines,
pines then cherish the circling wind—
so generous the moment.

*   *   *

On your knees, arms around your
four-year-old granddaughter—
beneath that baseball cap, your head
back, eyes closed,
an ecstatic tenderness
I've seen only on the face
of Bernini's Teresa.
I didn't know you until this photo.
What we don't see in those
we love, dear brother.

*   *   *

Outside the Avalon
a young man, perhaps
homeless, stares a long while
at a poster of Tom Hanks
as Fred Rogers on this
balmy winter's day
in the neighborhood.

*   *   *

Winter and autumn summer and
spring careen into and over each
other without direction from
millions of seasons before them.
Grieving and disoriented
I write this homage now a dirge
for the seasons we once knew
better than we know ourselves.

*   *   *

We prefer our greed to the mystery
of copper butterflies and horseshoe crabs.
We prefer our greed to prayer.
We can buy what we want.
Greenland or air.

*   *   *

A beetle clings to the
front screen. I flick it
away and it screams—
a trace of her life remains.
For a moment the entire world
is anguished by my hand.

*   *   *

Your brave struggles with
depression since we were small
remind me every day
even when fearful
never to turn away from
the suffering of others.

*　　*　　*

The silence
of
February
roars
expanding

the sky

*　　*　　*

The sun in one hand
and the moon in the other,
galaxies warm against
my awed heart,
I find my way.

*　　*　　*

As a child I saw only
your terrible stinginess.
I too was too unhappy
to reach out.
I'm still here but
you have passed on.
Dad, forgive me
take my hand
reach back.

*　　*　　*

Innumerable worlds
of unfathomable dimensions
of compassion help her
pour a glass of cool water
for her ailing mother.

*　　*　　*

Trees wave to the wind,
ferns nod and sway.
The wandering years wave too.
Hello, hello.
Hello and goodbye!
replies the wind.

Make a Little Music

In the distance
frogs croak in the mountain rice fields.
The evening's single song.

      –Ryokan, *One Robe, One Bowl*

In easing darkness
bird cries awaken
each shaft of ascending light
in tints of orange and rose
each shaft of cerise and peach.
Suddenly light is renewed.
Morning is strong and straight.

    *   *   *

So vast the sea
and its lucifactions
gulls see it always
for the first time.
Throats hoarse
and amazed
they cry over and
over, *The sea!*
The sea!

    *   *   *

In the sound of rain
the silence of sky and cloud winds
with the shredding tumble-
down of the sea.
Fresh and lonely
the rain is always
headed
home.

* * *

Alighting on a white fence
near a tree and a child's bicycle
on a summer morning a crow,
a shattering darkness, a hole
cut out of creation

and everything around it
receded and the heart stopped.
Unknowable our lives.

* * *

The whistle wails its imperative
to connect but we hurtle by
quiet fields rivers planets,
passing people I will never
know and might have loved.

* * *

The starling opens its beak
in startling heat and
staggers this way and that
over the wilting vinca,
not knowing what to do.
The robin stands immobile
with crusted eyes
only a blink of light.

*   *   *

Torrents of rain lash the trees
as lightning serrates light
and thunder howls.
The storm and the memory
of other summer storms
over so many years
an inexplicable sadness.

*   *   *

Put down words
pick up the tin whistle
from Dublin I tell myself.
Make a little music
however awful.

*   *   *

Inisheer, etched
by wind and *grykes*
from the crashing sea.
Light and free, I walk
stone-walled paths beyond
the length of time.

*   *   *

Silence whispers,
human being?
Don't know.
Don't know.
Who are you?
Don't know.
Don't know.

*   *   *

Offering incense with monks
at Eiheiji's main altar—
here the sky bows
and says its prayers.

*   *   *

I relax on the afternoon light
with poems written on Earth while a girl
maneuvers her kayak around the Pleiades.
Whatever is down there is up here.

*   *   *

Transported at the Ryokan Museum—
calligraphy brushed with twigs
his poems lofty and direct.
Then I see *temari* balls for sale
and smile when Ryokan with
wide sleeves tosses one
to me.

*   *   *

On the arm of the wind the long grass walks
up the hill and pauses for the view.
Then with exceeding courtesy the wind again
escorts the grass as they descend.

*   *   *

In the cool breezes
of summer
one eternity
after
another.

*   *   *

Thinner than a petal,
tending her garden
my sister says,
"I like to see things grow."
Every day I wonder
if she will be here
tomorrow
but then she tells me
about the okra.

~49~

*   *   *

En route
through scores of worlds
the sun sets in turquoise
over Uranus and on Earth
pauses at the end of the street
stunned by the beauty
clear and close-up
before finally rising.

*   *   *

"You never needed a mother,"
she said, overwhelmed
by my ill sister and
for mother gave me
rivers and mornings
and even more lovely
forgiveness.

*   *   *

Summer is crammed with light
like childhood and old age.
Our lives are August light
a perfect exhalation into splendor.

*   *   *

Sitting bench, light and strong,
you fold into my small suitcase.
We sat together at Dogen's temple
surrounded by towering cedars—
deep bows, kind friend.

*   *   *

We breathe together
and do not want.
There are just enough
breaths for everyone.

*   *   *

From overhead wires the drawn-
out lament of the mourning
dove for the late dawn
at the end of summer.

*   *   *

Breezes
light
on face
and
hands
here
here and
here
gone
forever.

TRAVELING THE LIGHT

Traveling the Light

A traveler—
This is what I shall be called.
—Matsuo Bashō, Travel Writings

But do not ask where I am going
As I travel in this limitless world
Where every step I take is my home.
—The Zen Poetry of Dogen

I
Starting Out

This June morning our breath stands tall
and we open to everything around us

underway on Belt Road in Northwest DC.
We travel through the wisdom of greens

and sunlight ringing like bells. Roof tiles
and stone walls also proceed and say hello then

turn with us onto Jenifer near a brick house
dingy with age and decay that joins too.

Zelkovas, red maples, and magnolias stroll to stretch
their legs. They explore the limits of the sky

when another sky appears and treks with them.
No keeping up with those long legs.

On 41st Street cirrus, tranquil and free, follow high above.
Unimagined realms flow through us.

A mockingbird stares at a massing of marigolds.
"Why is my song coming from the flowers?"

A small pile of fur from something dead roams
with us and the modest grass lingers

singing with the bees and grasshoppers it shades.
Marigolds bow to trash cans and a pair of old boots.

All of life steps over a garden hose and the hose
and matted clover wander too.

"Morning," says a man on his phone, exercising his dog
who lumbers beside him, both meandering along.

The crow's raucous clacks and rattlings fall over
roses alarmed that suddenly run after us.

Laughing, a woman in a red t-shirt retrieves her paper
and turns back to the intimate reaches of her home.

As we swing onto Harrison, suddenly the wind kicks
up and a boy comforts his crying brother and the wind.

Our peripatetic lives—a vanishing into vanishing
like clouds. At the corner of Belt a *shōdō* of lilies curves

toward the road on its way—a shower of yellow.
We ramble toward the rise ahead.

Whirligigs jig in a yard on Garrison as we climb
to 39th Street, decorous boxwood breaking free.

We see houses without porches that look forlorn
unable to welcome or protect their guests.

And a fox low to the ground trots into the dense
hydrangea of a yard, squirrel in its mouth.

Sunlight falls on an abused cat left out all night.
The sun and the cat lean into each other.

The wonder of walking on the great Earth—
stillness moves through a million

spinning worlds without ceasing.

II

Reaching Fort Reno Park

We cross the street to Fort Reno, the highest natural
point in the city, and traverse the narrow trail.

Under our feet the wounds of centuries. We step softly,
trying not to leave further harm. A man stooped

wearing a cheap glove grasps the crook of his cane.
His presence so quiet his face disappears.

I pass close to a woman who resembles my mother.
A great loneliness that lifted after she died

returns. I invite my mother to join me.
We free each other of many difficulties.

God walks too and delights in talking to the open fields
and to the dotted smartweed and wild rye.

Shouts from boys playing baseball. Rugged junipers
near a chain-link fence turn to look. Someone hits a home

run! Blue jays gasp. The crowd thrilled treasures the crack in time.
On a sidewalk close by, a girl on a skateboard—

passing each other we exchange faces. I'm on the
skateboard and she's ambling. Several boys rush pell-mell

out of the school. I remember the boys under Mylar in cages.
Even "deleted family units" walk with us.

Circling the park, I'm back to 39th Street, turning
turning and turning this cool morning, the warm unfolding

of life. No one, no thing is left behind.

III

Crossing to 39th, then Huntington

Traveling the light, we bring no destination.
Awareness pares to walking.

Is there anything that does not travel? Even light
sets out, one foot in front, one foot behind.

If light stops walking, the wind and curbs cease walking
and if the wind halts, we halt, water stops singing in the

streams and coursing beneath the ground. If the trees stop
reaching toward blue, we lose heart and the ants too

and the sound of a mower starting up would not rattle
like a loose chain, the Jack Russell barking would fall silent

and the heady scent of honeysuckle from its lively
trumpets would remain unheard.

We move west onto Huntington, a vagabond too.
All things migrate like the snow goose

suspended from my front porch blown
about by boreal winds over mountains and seas.

Hostas drift, widening their arc of attention. A teenager
pushes her friend who looks down and turns away.

A conference of signs? *Congratulations, Class of '22,
Statehood for DC, Two-Hour Parking*—green letters

on cream. An arrow for a one-way street.
Hate Has No Home Here, the loveliest flower

in that front yard in these dark days. Signs rove
along with a gas grill, lawn chairs, and phrases of Spanish.

Rickety chairs pass quickly before I can snag one.
Back spent, I sit down on a neighbor's wall and smile—

our intertwined and ever-changing lives.

IV

Turning Toward Home

We walk without walking, until the path drops
away. Like the breath we cling to nothing.

The footfalls of walking are never ending—
we are ever right here.

Veering north onto 41st Street, we glimpse our home
and at once make out the fiery wines and golds

of autumn, the icy branches of January oaks,
white dogwoods, and the scorch of summers.

The four seasons are here and their weathers.
Past, present, and future are here. The sun and the lonely

phases of the moon meet at last. Every joy
and suffering we encountered on the road is here.

Which were joys? Which sufferings?
Don't know.

I see my father, my mother! And the murmur
of lilacs whose fragrance she loved.

Inconceivable life and I go down into the roots
of trees and up toward the constellations.

The stars walk with us and all beings, pointing out
the sights, and we offer the warm stars

the marvels on Earth, a freshness
beyond life and death, heaven and earth.

Here in eternity, beyond eternity—
no boundaries together we enter

this very moment.

ACKNOWLEDGMENTS

Profound gratitude and love to Roshi Robert Jinsen Kennedy, S.J., from whom I received Dharma transmission. Beyond his rigorous teaching, he always found time to encourage my poetry. Every two weeks for over a decade, I jumped on the Vamoose bus in DC and headed toward Morning Star Zendo in Jersey City. My debt is immeasurable.

My first Zen teacher, Roshi Janet Jinne Richardson, CSJP, co-founder of Clare Sangha, read much of my poetry and was always supportive. I practiced with her and Sensei Rosalie Jishin McQuaide, CSJP, in Baltimore. Their friendship is a treasure.

These poems were written over the period that coincided with the growth of Sky Above Great Wind, inspired by the Japanese poet-monk Ryokan. These were vital years of designing the website, finding a congenial place to sit, and growing a small and committed sangha. My warmest, wholehearted thanks to everyone.

I am especially indebted to Rennie McQuilkin, publisher of Antrim House. What a great pleasure to work with him.

Special thanks to my sister Deborah and to my brother James, who lives in the North Carolina mountains. They provide the life-affirming constancy of love, memory, and family.

There are no words to express my joy for Karin and our thirty-five years of reading and writing, travel, and wonder. Without her unfailing generosity, Sky Above would not have gotten off the ground and this book would not be in your hands now. Her delight in words adds light, clarity, and play to each page. Boundless gratitude.

ABOUT THE AUTHOR

Susan Lynn KōDō Efird, Sensei, is from Winston-Salem, North Carolina. She is the author of the book-length poem *The Eye of Heaven* with wood engravings by Michael McCurdy (Harry Duncan, Abattoir Editions) and shorter poems that appeared in *Poetry, Southern Poetry Review, Verve, JAMA, A Garland for Harry Duncan,* and other publications. Her lifelong immersion in literature and service began with an entry-level position at *The New Yorker.* She has worked as a volunteer for hospice, AIDS, and Alzheimer's patients, with prisoners through Lifelines to Solitary, as well as serving as aide to bird keepers at the National Zoo. For many years before her retirement, she was senior writer-editor at the Smithsonian American Art Museum. She is the founder and guiding teacher of Sky Above Great Wind, and a member of the White Plum Asanga. She lives in Washington, D.C.

This book is set in Garamond Premier Pro, which originated in 1988 when type-designer Robert Slimbach visited the Plantin-Moretus Museum in Antwerp, Belgium, to study its collection of Claude Garamond's metal punches and typefaces. During the 1500s Garamond—a Parisian punch-cutter—produced a refined array of book types that combined an unprecedented degree of balance and elegance, for centuries standing as the pinnacle of beauty and practicality in type-founding. They were based on the handwriting of Angelo Vergecio, court librarian of the French king, Francis I. Slimbach has created a new interpretation based on Garamond's designs and on compatible italics cut by Robert Granjon, Garamond's contemporary.

Copies of this book can be ordered
from all bookstores and Amazon.

•

For more information on the work of Susan Kōdō Efird
visit www.antrimhousebooks.com/authors.html.